Debbie Duncan's books are a word in season, speaking directly into our anxious culture. She retells Bible stories through the lens of emotion, in a lively and accessible way. The brilliant, two-tiered approach means that both little ones and older children alike will come away with a greater grasp of their emotional and mental well-being.

Katharine Hill, UK Director of Care for the Family

Adults and children will find this series thought-provoking and encouraging in ~~~ ~~~ ~~~ h feelings. We often ᵢ ᵢ s that help childr em, are an invalua ell-being.

*Sue Monckt~~~ ~~~tian
Counsellors*

Despite the increased focus on mental well-being around us, we rarely consider the emotional challenges of characters in the Bible. And yet, their feelings and responses are so helpful for us as we navigate our own obstacles and opportunities. This series gives parents and adults the tools to dig deeper with children and young people, enabling them to relate and learn from the valuable truths and experiences found in these much loved stories. These books will build emotional resilience and strong faith — and are great fun to read. What's not to love?

*Cathy Madavan, Speaker, author, and Kyria Network
board member*

May this encourage you Debbie

Debbie Duncan's *God Cares* series brilliantly helps children understand the emotions of Bible characters while encouraging them to explore their own emotions in the face of similar situations. What is more, the books do it in a style that retains the excitement and adventure of the stories themselves. The books also offer practical help to parents and carers as they engage with their children on this voyage of discovery.

Bob Hartman, *Author and performance storyteller*

According to Barnardo's one in ten children have a diagnosable mental health condition and many, while they are undiagnosed, are unhappy and anxious for many reasons in today's world. Early intervention is vital before their feelings become more problematic. Debbie's *God Cares* series offers a gentle in-road for parents and carers to encourage them to open up about what they are feeling and what is going on in their lives. Learning early on how much God loves them and cares for them can only be a positive. Seeing their own feelings in well-known Bible characters will show them that no matter what the circumstance, God always wins!

Karen Lennie, *Cognitive Behavioural Psychotherapist PG Dip BABCP Member (Accred)*

GOD CARES

WHEN LIFE IS TOUGH

Paul and
Other Stories

By Debbie Duncan

CANDLE
BOOKS

Lucas – you have a gift, keep writing!
And I am celebrating having grandchildren
– Arthur and baby Arnold.

Text copyright © 2021 Debbie Duncan
This edition copyright © 2021 Lion Hudson IP Limited

The right of Debbie Duncan to be identified as the author of this work has
been asserted by her in accordance with the Copyright, Designs and Patents
Act 1988.

Published by
Lion Hudson Limited
Wilkinson House, Jordan Hill Business Park
Banbury Road, Oxford OX2 8DR, England
www.lionhudson.com

ISBN 978 1 78128 399 8

First edition 2021

Acknowledgments
Cover illustration by Anita Belli
Scripture quotations taken from the Holy Bible, New International Version
Anglicised. Copyright 1979, 1984, 2011 Biblica, formerly International Bible
Society. Used by permission of Hodder & Stoughton Ltd, an Hachette UK
company. All rights reserved. "NIV" is a registered trademark of Biblica. UK
trademark number 1448790.

The quotation on p.6 is taken from *Aspire* magazine.

A catalogue record for this book is available from the British Library
Printed and bound in China, February 2021, LH54

CONTENTS

About the Series

"In raising healthy children, it's not enough to just focus on the physical aspect of health. To be truly healthy, a child's emotional health must be nurtured and strengthened. Developing a mental attitude of wellness is also essential. When we adopt an attitude of wellness, we take on a belief that being well is a natural, normal state."

Jane Sheppard, "A Wellness Approach for Children", *Aspire* **magazine, 9 June 2009**

The *God Cares* series is about providing parents with a biblical approach to discussing emotions and behaviour with their children to provide an attitude of wellness. Children of different ages and at different stages of their emotional development approach things differently, so this series works on two separate levels: **readers aimed at five- to seven-year olds, and chapter books aimed at children aged eight and above**. Please note that children progress at different rates in terms of their reading ability and emotional development, so the age ranges are only a guide for parents and carers.

The Bible stories are retold reflecting on the emotions. Children are encouraged to discuss this and relate the stories to their own situations. Sections at the back provide a reflective space for children, and practical advice for parents and carers.

About the Author

Debbie Duncan, the author of *The Art of Daily Resilience* and *Brave*, is a nurse, a teacher, and the mother of four children. Debbie has considerable insight into what constitutes resilience and bravery: the ability to cope, to stay on course, and to bounce back. In her books she considers what is required for physical, mental, and spiritual durability, interweaving biblical teaching and prayers with personal anecdotes and sound advice. This she now applies specifically to support parents and carers raising children.

Introduction

The Bible was written many hundreds of years ago. God used different people to write it but they were inspired or helped by God to write it. That is why even today the stories and parables in it help us to make sense of the world we live in.

One of the writers of many of the books in the second part of the Bible was a man known as Saul, who later God called Paul. In this book, we will call him Saul until the time in the story when his name was changed. At the start of our story, we hear how Saul hated those who believed in Jesus so much that he journeyed hundreds of miles to capture them, throw them in jail, or even murder them. Later, in an amazing event, Saul came face to face with Jesus, and his whole life changed. He became known as Paul, and he grew to be one of the greatest teachers the church has ever known.

Saul lived in Israel during a time when the Romans ruled the land. Their ruler was a cruel man named Nero. Nero is thought to have burnt down his own city, Rome, so he could rebuild it the way he wanted it while blaming the fire on the Christians. He did not care about the people and their homes as he watched the city burn. These were challenging and difficult times.

Throughout these pages, we will discover how Paul endured many difficult things because he believed in Jesus. People hit him with sticks, and later with stones; he was thrown into prison; and he suffered hunger, thirst, and cold because he believed in Jesus. He was also shipwrecked – not once or twice, which would have been scary, but three times! What an extraordinary life. At the end of his life, Paul was imprisoned for a long time and finally murdered for his faith by Nero. Paul knew that believing in Jesus would not be easy, but he believed that Jesus was and is worth serving, even though it meant he would have a tough life. Paul knew that God cared for him and would never leave him.

After reading the story, discuss it, and how you feel, with your parents or those who care for you. There are some talking points at the end of the book to help you.

CHAPTER ONE

LET'S MEET PAUL

Paul lived an extraordinary life. He is quite famous, even though he lived hundreds of years ago. He was born in a place called Tarsus, which was a bustling trading city in a country known today as Turkey.

Saul, as he was known in his early life, had a good education. Not everyone at that time was able to go to school, or learn how to read and write. Saul was taught by the best teachers. He was also taught about God and would have had to memorize large portions of the older part of the Bible. As he grew older, Saul learnt how to make tents. This was a good job to have, as tents were more popular then than they are now. A lot of people lived in one if they could not afford a house. It also meant Saul could work anywhere. (This would be very useful later on, when he made long journeys across many countries to tell people about Jesus. It meant he could always get work, and pay for somewhere to sleep and for his food.)

In his early years, Saul was a member of the Pharisees, which was a religious group that focused on tradition rather than listening to what God says. The Pharisees were a group of Jewish people who wanted to follow God's law found in the Ten Commandments and in the early books of the Bible. They were so afraid of failing God that they added lots of other rules around God's commandments. They were so obsessed about not breaking any of God's rules that they forgot about God's love.

Jesus often tried to explain to the Pharisees that God loved them. One day, he went into the synagogue (the Pharisees' place of worship) and a man with a damaged hand was there. Some of the Pharisees were watching Jesus carefully in case he broke one of their rules. It was because it was their Sabbath, the day in the week when they were meant to worship God. The problem was they had so many rules about that day that people were more worried about breaking the rules than worshipping God.

Jesus was more concerned about the man with the damaged hand. He made him stand up, and then asked everyone a question: on the Sabbath day, was it more important to do good and save someone than to kill someone? He asked the question looking at the Pharisees, saddened that they were more concerned about rules than showing God's love and compassion.

Jesus asked the man to hold out his

hand, which had been completely healed. Jesus had done good, he had saved someone. The Pharisees left angry and determined to find a way to kill Jesus.

This story can be found in the New Testament in Mark chapter 3, verses 1–6.

~~~~~~

Saul and the Pharisees did not believe that Jesus was the Son of God. Anyone saying that could be arrested or even killed. After Jesus' death, Saul was ordered by the Pharisees to stop the newly formed Christian church from growing by any means possible. That even meant killing one of the followers of Jesus, a man named Stephen. Saul thought that everyone who followed the way of Jesus Christ should be arrested and possibly face the death penalty. He dragged men, women, and children to prison because they believed in Jesus.

Many of these new believers left Jerusalem where they had seen Jesus killed and rise from the dead. This city had become the centre of the church but it was also a dangerous place to live. Many fled from the capital to other cities like Damascus, which was 140 miles (225 km) from Jerusalem. The Bible describes Saul as "breathing out murderous threats against the Lord's disciples" (Acts 9:1). He went to the Jewish leaders and asked for letters proving who he was so that he could give them to the authorities in Damascus.

Have you ever felt you were in a difficult situation because others hold different views? Try writing down how you felt in the box on the next page, and then share what you have written with someone you trust.

CHAPTER TWO

ON THE ROAD TO DAMASCUS

Saul thought he knew God and tried to obey all the traditions of his faith. He became so obsessed with carrying out the traditions and following the additional rules that people had made that he lost sight of who God really is. He was not listening to God, but God knew how to get his attention. God had to speak to Saul in a dramatic way to make him listen.

As Saul was heading to the city of Damascus, a sudden light from heaven flashed around him.

Can you imagine how scared Saul and even his horse must have been? It was so dramatic that Saul fell to the ground. He may have hurt himself as he fell but he didn't care about that. He was listening to a voice calling his name even though the light had blinded him. This was a man who usually had no fear. He chased people he thought were criminals and was not afraid of anything. This man fell to his knees in fear.

He heard a voice saying, "Saul, Saul, why do you persecute me?" Persecute means to badly treat, hurt, or oppress someone.

Saul did not understand what was happening, but he knew of stories in the Old Testament when God called people by their name.

~~~~~~~~~~~~~~~~~~~~~~~~~~~~~~

God has called many people by their name to get their attention. One of the stories in the Old Testament is that of Samuel, who had to listen to God.

Before Samuel was born, his mother, Hannah, was married but was unable to have any children and this made her very sad. One day, Hannah went up to the place where she worshipped God and prayed with all her heart that God would answer her prayer. The priest heard the noise she was making and thought she was drunk! Hannah explained why she was so sad, and the priest prayed with her. God answered Hannah's prayer and she had a son. Sometimes our prayers are not answered and we don't know why, but on this occasion Hannah's prayer was answered.

Hannah named her son Samuel, which means "Heard by God". As a thank you to God, Hannah asked the priest to bring up Samuel when he was older so that he could work for God. So Samuel went to live with the priest named Eli.

One night, Eli and Samuel had gone to bed when Samuel heard someone call his name. He ran to Eli and said, "Here I am; you called me." But Eli told Samuel he hadn't called him, and told the boy to go back to bed. The same thing happened again – and again Eli told Samuel to go back to bed. When it happened a third time, Samuel got up and went to Eli and said, "Here I am; you called me." Eli realized that the Lord was calling Samuel and told him to lie down and answer God by saying, "Speak, Lord, for your servant is listening." Samuel did as Eli suggested and the Lord God told Samuel what he was going to do to help the people in Israel. Samuel kept listening to God and served him.

You can read the full story in 1 Samuel chapters 1 and 3.

God speaks to us today in lots of ways. You may not hear him call your name but the Bible tells us that he calls us his children if we follow him. Sometimes, when life is tough, we forget to listen to God and think he is not listening. He is listening and is always ready to hear our prayers.

Blinded by the light, Saul knew God was calling his name. He asked, "Who are you, Lord?"

The reply from heaven was, "I am Jesus of Nazareth, whom you are persecuting." Jesus told Saul to get up and head into the city of Damascus, and there he would be told what to do. The men that were journeying with Saul were also amazed at what had happened. They too had seen the light and heard the voice from heaven. Saul got up from the ground and realized that he was unable to see. He must have found that very scary but the people who were with him helped him to go to Damascus.

In Damascus, Saul met a man named Ananias who loved Jesus. Ananias was warned by God that Saul was coming to the city but that he now followed Jesus and would need his help. Can you imagine having to help your worst enemy? Not only did Ananias help Saul, but he also prayed for him and Saul was healed. I think Ananias was a brave man, as he must have known that Saul had been chasing and even killing people he knew because of their faith in Jesus.

Saul's sight returned. He had a new heart to serve God, and he stayed in Damascus and shared his story with the Christians who lived there. They were amazed that this man, who had once hunted them to kill them, now served God. Saul told everyone he met about Jesus – that he was the Son of God, and that he died taking our punishment so that we could know God better. Saul told everyone that following all the rules was not as important as believing that Jesus died so that God could forgive us.

The Jewish people who lived in Damascus were shocked by the change in Saul. They decided to kill Saul to stop him telling people about Jesus. Saul's friends heard about the plot, so they got a huge basket and made Saul climb into it. They then lowered Saul over the city wall, so he didn't have to go through the main gate where his enemies were waiting to kill him. Saul then headed to Jerusalem a changed man. He knew that becoming a Christian would mean he was in danger, but he had come to know Jesus and decided that was more important than even his own life. From then on, Saul was named Paul. It was a new name for a man who now served God and loved Jesus, not one who persecuted him.

CHAPTER THREE

PAUL'S THREE LONG JOURNEYS

When Paul first went to Jerusalem, the Christians who lived there were afraid of him. They even wondered if he pretended to believe in Jesus so he could capture them. This was a difficult time. The king of Israel was King Herod Agrippa and he worked for the Roman rulers and did not like the Christians. He killed Jesus' brother James, and even had Jesus' disciple Peter imprisoned. Later,

Paul was also put in prison. In fact, during the thirty-five years in which Paul served Jesus and the church, we know he was arrested three times. I expect it happened more times than that, but the Bible only tells us about some of the tough things Paul went through.

~~~~~~

Peter was one of Jesus' closest friends. He knew what Jesus had done for us and understood it was good news. In fact, he was so excited about this good news that he shared it with as many people as he could. King Herod Agrippa imprisoned Peter and decided he was going to kill him. While Peter was in prison, the church prayed asking God's help for him to be released. They were very serious about praying for Peter and some people even stopped eating for a few days.

The night before Peter was going to die, he was chained up in his prison cell. There were two soldiers on the other side of the door guarding him. I am sure Peter was afraid but he had to trust God. Suddenly an angel appeared to Peter in the middle of his prison cell. He poked Peter and told him to wake up. Peter must have been confused and frightened. As he got up, the chains fell off him. The angel told Peter to put on his shoes and coat, and follow him. Peter did as he was told. He was so confused he thought he was dreaming. They walked out of the cell, past the two huge sleeping soldiers, to the big iron gate leading into the city. The gate opened and Peter found himself walking along a lane. The angel disappeared and Peter probably had to pinch himself to prove he really was awake.

Peter headed to Mary's house. Her maid heard Peter calling, opened the door, and was amazed. She tried to tell everyone that Peter was there but they all thought she was mad. However, when they eventually came to the door, they were shocked to see it was true. Their prayers had been answered. (Just imagine the trouble the soldiers would be in as their valuable prisoner had escaped!)

This story can be found in Acts chapter 12, verses 1–16.

Paul made three long journeys during his lifetime, to start new churches or to visit existing churches so he could encourage them. If all the miles he walked were added up, it would probably come to around 10,000 miles (16,000 km). That is like walking from London to the North Pole nearly four times!

Paul's first journey took quite a few years. He headed to Cyprus by boat with his friends Barnabas and John Mark. When Paul arrived, he taught people about Jesus. There was a Jewish false prophet called Bar-Jesus who worked for the rulers of the town and lied about Paul and God's teachings. Bar-Jesus didn't want people becoming Christians as that would mean they would not follow him. Paul told the man that he was making crooked the straight paths of God, and caused him to be blind for a while. After the ruler of Cyprus saw what had happened and understood God's power, he turned to God.

After the three men left Cyprus, John Mark returned to Jerusalem while Paul and Barnabas went to a place called Antioch. Once again, they told the people about Jesus but the Jews became jealous of them and tried to harm them. However, Paul did not worry about this as he knew God was with them. Paul and Barnabas continued their work together and the church grew in numbers. Often, they left the places they were in as people plotted against them. In one town called Lystra, Paul healed a disabled man and everyone was amazed. However, the Jewish people encouraged the crowd to believe Paul and Barnabas were bad men, and Paul was stoned, almost to death.

Finally, after a time preaching in Lystra, Paul and Barnabas returned to Antioch. Along the way they stopped at the towns of Derbe, Iconium, and Attila. Paul and Barnabas eventually returned to the church in Antioch, where they were able to share all the amazing things that had happened to them. They stayed there for a long time with the people who loved Jesus. In tough times, rest is important and God provides this. They journeyed over 1,200 miles (1,900 km) and it took them several years. It was just as well that Paul could make and repair tents to earn money as the trip must have been expensive.

They spent some time in Antioch recovering before they set sail and headed out on another huge journey. Paul wrote to his friend Timothy and told him that he had a really difficult time. He never really said much about all the tough things he went through. Paul wanted people in the church to know that no matter how hard life could be, knowing God is with us means we can stay strong and have courage for each day. It means we can be joyful and know we are loved, even though we are living through difficult times.

After a rest, Paul then decided he wanted to visit and help the Christians that he had seen during his first long trip. Paul took his friend Silas with him this time, and Barnabas and John Mark went in a different direction. Paul's second missionary journey took three years. He even returned to Damascus, but once again he was given a tough time by the people who did not believe in Jesus. In one of the places Paul and Silas journeyed to, they were imprisoned for causing too much trouble, even though they were trying to help someone. Their belongings were taken off them and they were even beaten with whips. They were then thrown into prison, probably scared, bleeding, and in pain. The jailer told the soldiers to watch Paul and Silas carefully. These soldiers put chains on their feet so they could not move. I wonder if they had heard the story of Peter and how he had escaped from prison. The soldiers probably thought, "There is no way these two are going to escape!"

Instead of thinking about how awful things were, Paul and Silas started praying and singing songs to God. They were able to turn to God for strength in the middle of a really difficult time. It seemed life could not get any worse than this, and then there was an earthquake! What would you do? There was nowhere to take cover. The earthquake was so powerful that even the prison walls shook. As a result, all the doors were opened and Silas and Paul found that their chains were loose. But they did not escape and they told the other prisoners not to escape either.

The jailer was so scared when he woke up and found that the prisoners' chains were loose. He knew he could be killed if they escaped, but he was amazed to see they were still all there. Paul and Silas were able to tell the jailer and his family about God's love, and they all became Christians. The two men had followed God in a difficult time and their example was like a light spreading God's goodness to others.

The ruler decided to let Paul and Silas go free when he realized Paul was a Roman citizen. In those days, a Roman citizen was not allowed to be whipped or tortured, and had to be treated respectfully in prison. Paul and Silas journeyed through many countries and finally made it back to Antioch where they stayed for a while. They must have been exhausted, as so much had happened to them. They then had to make the long journey back to their homes. I expect they slept for ages when they finally got there!

Paul reminds us to trust God. He did not know what would happen when he and Silas were put in jail, but they decided to trust God. We may think things will never change. Have you ever felt like you are in prison like Paul and Silas? We can trust God for his care and protection. Sometimes he answers our prayers in an amazing way!

CHAPTER FOUR

PAUL'S FINAL JOURNEY

Paul's third journey was a longer trip than the previous two. He went back to places he had visited on his first two journeys, encouraging the churches and visiting friends. The book of Acts in the Bible tells us that he spent a lot of his time in an ancient city port called Ephesus. Paul told the people about Jesus but some of them were worried that if people started to follow Jesus, they would stop buying statues of the made-up Greek gods. One man, who had made a lot of money by selling these statues, was furious that he would lose sales. He stirred up the people's anger, telling them lies and confusing them. Paul had to leave and went on to visit other towns and cities on his last long journey. There were some places Paul wanted to go to, but he found out they were unsafe to visit.

Paul headed back to Jerusalem but there he was beaten. People lied about what he had done, so he was imprisoned, and moved from prison to prison. He also stood before lots of different rulers, who were unsure of what to do with him. Paul had Roman citizenship because he was born in Tarsus, which was a free city in Rome. This meant he had more rights than other Jewish people, and he was entitled to a legal trial where people would have to listen to what he had to say.

Paul must have been exhausted from all his trips and scared by the way people treated him. However, he did not focus on the bad things that were going on but decided to remind himself of how much God loved him. Paul told everyone he met about God's love. He was moved from jail to jail for about two whole years! Paul didn't get angry or say anything unkind about those who treated him badly.

Eventually, the Roman rulers decided to send Paul to Rome in the country of Italy, which was the capital of their lands. It was the city where all the big decisions were made and where the main court was. Some of the people wanted to kill Paul but they could only do this by accusing him of treason. Others were unsure what to do. Jerusalem was quite a distance from Rome. If you go by plane today it would take you three and a half hours — that's half a day at school!

So Paul was taken with a lot of other prisoners and put on a boat that would sail from Israel to Italy. The journey in those days would usually take over a month. The soldier in charge, a kind centurion, let Paul's friends stay with him before they set sail.

They were at sea for quite a long time. The journey seemed to take longer than it should have and then they were caught in a violent storm. I expect the prisoners were fed up. I wonder if some of them were seasick? It must have been an awful journey for them all.

The sailors would have been concerned about

everyone's safety as the waves crashed into the boat. Paul tried to warn them that they should find a safe harbour to stop but they wanted to keep going. Things became even worse when a few days later the ship was hit by another storm. This time the waves were so high and the storm so strong that the sailors had to throw all the people's belongings overboard into the sea. It must have been so frightening, but Paul had lived through many tough things and he knew God was with him. Even in the darkest days, Paul believed nothing is too difficult for God to overcome.

The strong winds blew and the sun disappeared from view. Everyone thought they were going to die. They also had very little food as it had been thrown overboard. They were hungry and in the dark, and I expect they were frightened. Paul stood up and told them they should have listened to what he had to say. He said God had sent an angel who told him no one would die and that God would protect them. He told them about the God he knew and trusted. Again, Paul's life was like a light to those around him. Paul's strength and courage in the tough situation helped give encouragement to the others on board.

Can you think of a time when things were tough and you did not know what to do? Draw a picture in just pencil of the last time things were tough. After you have done this, add some colour showing where God was in this situation.

This is extra space for you to draw in.

After two weeks at sea, the sailors thought they were near land. They decided to escape from the ship, but Paul warned them that they had to stay together. He told them to eat what little food they had left as he knew this would give them courage and strength. Even when things are tough, we still need to eat and sleep. We do need to look after ourselves. So, the 276 people on the boat all had something to eat and then rested.

The next morning, they looked out and saw a beach. They were excited to see land. While they were trying to work out what to do, the ship hit sand and got stuck. The soldiers wanted to kill all the prisoners, but Paul told everyone who could swim to jump in the sea and swim for shore, and anyone else should follow by clinging onto planks and other pieces of the ship. All the sailors, prisoners, and soldiers reached the land safely as God had promised them, even though they had a tough time getting there. This was the island known as Malta.

Just after they arrived, poor exhausted Paul was bitten by a venomous snake hiding in wood that he had collected for a fire. The local people thought maybe he was a bad man and deserved the punishment, but Paul was not harmed by the snake. They then wondered if he was a man of faith. The local people provided the sailors, soldiers, and prisoners with what they needed to keep journeying on because they wanted to thank Paul for healing one of their leaders. Paul was able to show and tell the people of the island about God.

This was not the end of Paul's journey. It took several more months for him to reach Rome. When he finally arrived, he was imprisoned in his own home for several years. He did not stop telling people about Jesus and how much God loves us. Even though Paul was a prisoner, he was still like a light encouraging others to be kind to one another.

Jesus used images to help people understand his teachings. He said we are to be as salt and light. In those days, salt was very valuable as people used it for many different things such as for cleaning wounds or preserving food.

You only need a tiny bit of salt when tasting it. That is the same as light. Have you ever been in a dark room and you move the curtains a little bit? The room fills with light. Jesus tells us to be like salt and light in the world so that people can see what his followers are like, and know that God cares for us and helps us. Even our smallest actions and words can make a difference. Paul's life was like this.

This story is found in Matthew chapter 5, verses 13–16.

Paul had journeyed many miles teaching people about Jesus, and helping and supporting the church. During his travels and his years imprisoned in Rome, Paul wrote many letters to the churches and his friends. People think that Paul wrote 13 of the 27 books of the second part of the Bible called the New Testament. That means he probably wrote nearly half of it. Although he wrote the letters and books that are part of the Bible, God helped him to do it.

Some people think that Paul made a fourth trip to Spain, which was over 3,000 miles (4,800 km) away.

Paul lived an extraordinary life. He was put in jail at least four times, stoned, whipped, and badly injured. He was shipwrecked three times and bitten by a snake. He lived through some tough times, but he did not stop telling people about Jesus and how much God loves us. He also knew God was with him. Paul was able to share God's love with the people he met as he was changed so much by it.

What do you do when things get tough? When things became tough for Paul, he tried to think about what Jesus had done for him and talked to God. I think that is a good thing to do.

CHAPTER FIVE

WHAT YOU CAN DO

Learning about Paul and what he went through reminds us that even when things are tough, we can trust God. Paul lived a remarkable life and so many things happened to him. Sometimes we think life should be OK if we are good and love God but that is not true. Sometimes bad things happen to good people. The most important thing to remember is that God cares — God is with us even when life is tough.

I had a friend help me with this book called Lucas Dickson. He is young like you, aged seven years old. Lucas loves writing and this is what he told me about the life of Paul.

~~~~~~

Paul was a man who was born in Tarsus. Paul thought he was cooler than everyone else. He found out that he could get the people following Jesus put in jail. Paul thought he was doing good but one day God shone a light into Paul's eyes. He had been blinded by hate and learned to see the truth.

After he could see again, Paul decided he would follow Jesus and tell people about God. The people did not want to listen to Paul. They even tried to put him in jail. Paul didn't mind being in jail as he could tell people about Jesus. He didn't mind being put in jail, bullied, or even dying if he could tell people about Jesus. God was with Paul as he was bullied. One night, God sent an earthquake to open the gates of the jail. Paul stayed in jail for a while to tell the guard about Jesus. Paul was probably in jail at least four times, was shipwrecked three times, and bitten by a snake, but he was still happy as he knew God loved him.

~~~~~~~~~~~~~~~~~~~~

Talking Points

The following questions are here to help you think about the things we have read. They are ideas for you to chat about with your parents, a teacher, someone at church, or another adult you can trust.

Questions:
- How would you summarize Paul's story in 200 words?
- What did the young Saul believe was more important than knowing God?
- What did Saul do to the Christians that he met?
- Why do you think God blinded Saul for three days?
- What do you think Saul was afraid of?
- How did Saul's life change when he heard that

God loved him and had sent his son so that
Saul could really know God?
- Do you think Paul's life became easier after
  he became a Christian?
- How did God care and provide for Paul
  during tough times?
- What did Paul and Silas do after they were
  beaten, chained, and put in prison?

God spoke to Saul even when Saul was not
listening to him. He grabbed his attention and
showed him how Jesus was sent to save him.
Saul's whole life changed. Instead of capturing
Christians, throwing them into jail, or killing
them, the new Saul – now called Paul – spent
his life telling people about how much God loves
them. Despite having a tough time, he always
knew that God was with him. Paul could have
sat in the prison cell and cried about what was
happening. He could have sat in the ship and not
said a word. Paul could have been angry with the
people that tried to hurt him and he could have
run away. Instead Paul had a strong faith and
this helped him not to be angry with those who
were being unkind to him and not to be worried

about what might lie ahead. He felt able to help people that needed help, and to always thank God, no matter where he was, knowing that his situation was in God's hands.

We may not find ourselves in the same situation as Paul. Across the world today, however, there are many countries where people are imprisoned, beaten, and even die if they believe in Jesus. In our country, we are allowed to believe in God. Imagine if people told you that you could not believe in God? Of the 198 countries in the world, 52 countries such as China do not like Christians. They have laws and rules in place stopping people meeting in church, meeting together, or even having a Bible. We should pray for these people who do not have the freedoms we have.

You may not be shipwrecked, thrown in prison, or bitten by a snake, but bad things may happen to you. You might be bullied for the clothes you wear, for the way you speak, or even for what you believe in. You may be unwell or someone in your family could be sick. There are lots and lots of reasons why life can be tough. The following list suggests things that you can do when this is the case.

- Talk to people you trust about what is going on.
- Remember you are not alone. Even in a prison cell, Paul knew God was with him.
- Talk to God about what is going on. We can trust God, no matter how hard things are. Paul taught us this.
- Write a list to remind yourself of how God has helped you in the past.

On the next page is a prayer that you can pray. You may want to say your own prayer or write one down.

Prayer

Dear God,

Thank you that no matter the mistakes I make, you love me just like you loved Paul.

Thank you for reminding me that no matter how tough life can be, you are with me like you were with Paul.

You know everything about me from the number of hairs on my head to my favourite food. Help me to trust you and to talk to you about what is going on in my life.

Help me, too, to be able to tell other people about Jesus, your son, and be like salt and light for others.

Thank you that Jesus died for me. Thank you for this good news.

Amen.

Remember, God cares for you even when life is tough.

This is a space to write your prayers.

Chapter Six

PRACTICAL HELP

for Parents, Carers, and Teachers

By Sharon Morrison (SEN/Medical needs assistant) and Debbie Duncan

One of the most important things we can do for our children is to help them learn to cope with the difficulties of life. Stress, sadness, and disappointments are a natural part of people's lives. If children learn to cope while they are young, it means they will have the strength and confidence they need as they mature.

As parents, our natural instinct is to protect our children. We do not want them to be afraid or anxious. That means there are times that we don't tell them the truth, or we may believe that a lack of emotion is a sign of strength. So we teach them to be strong, enforcing this when they do not cry at emotional events. They try to be strong and show no emotion but we need to help them find a balance. We need to support our children to be open and transparent about how they feel as this will support their emotional well-being.

Children who deny their feelings are often trying to act tough – often to please an adult. This is not the same as being mentally strong. We need to be careful that we don't suppress their emotions. It is good to identify and label your child's feelings. This validates their emotions and helps them to recognize them. You are teaching them the difference between feelings and behaviour. You can teach them things like, "It's OK to feel afraid but it's not OK to try to hide."

We want them to know that bad things happen to good people. They are learning that life is tough, but we want to remind them that they are not alone. We also want to remind them that God can use our difficult experiences to help others. Although Paul was being taken to Rome on a ship to be put in prison, God used him to help all the soldiers and passengers on board when the ship hit a terrifying storm. They all survived the storm and reached land because of Paul's advice that was given to him through an angel. Share with your child or pupil how God has helped you in a difficult situation. Children can relate better to real situations.

Another example in the story is when Paul and his friend Silas were put in prison, and they experienced an earthquake that shook the prison and their chains fell off. They got to share their faith with the prison officer, and they led him and his family to God. Sometimes when our children face new situations, they can become anxious and fearful. Help them to understand that they are not alone and that God will always be with them. This could be when starting a new school, when changing classes or teachers, or when moving house, town, or even country.

Paul's circumstances changed so much as he was journeying, resting, or in prison, yet he still trusted God. Your child may have changing circumstances that can cause them anxiety and fear, especially when they don't understand why things are happening. Children are stronger than we think, and shielding them completely does not equip them for real life. The best gifts we can give them are our time and support in these difficult situations they face. Examples are losing a loved one or a family pet, a marriage break-up, or a rift in family relationships. We should involve our children when they are suffering and anxious, and help them through these changes, perhaps making a memory book with photos and drawings, or planting a plant that they can care for. They could also make a short film with photos and videos of their loved one.

Pray with your child using prayers of your own or those from a book. Often, adults remember the prayers that they prayed as children. Repetitive prayers and some rhyme prayers are helpful and bring peace to a child. This is the same with worship songs, which are accessible from websites like YouTube or Spotify. This can be a special time at bedtime as there are no distractions and many honest little chats can take place. I remember them well and now I have them with my grandchildren!

If things look like they will not change for a while, then help your children build a coping kit. This is a list of strategies that can help when things are tough. These can include:

- Eating well, and getting enough rest and sleep
- Relaxation therapy or deep breathing
- Taking regular exercise
- Keeping a journal
- Learning how to talk back to worries and reframe thoughts
- Talking to God
- Sharing with a child how God has helped you in a difficult situation. Children can relate better to real situations.
- Reminding a child they are not alone
- Supporting a child to do practical things to help them express their emotion
- Praying together
- Being open and honest about life
- Giving a child a sense of stability during a difficult time. This may include a regular

bedtime or a time when there are no distractions, which can facilitate honest conversations about life.
· Developing a coping kit, following the strategies above.

Ultimately every child is unique and every set of circumstances is unique. It may be that you will need to tailor the support you can give to the situation your child is going through. On the next page are some resources that may be helpful.

Resources

Care for the Family:
https://www.careforthefamily.org.uk/

Scripture Union:
https://content.scriptureunion.org.uk/resources-activities

The National Society for the Prevention of Cruelty to Children (NSPCC) have some helpful articles on their website:
https://www.nspcc.org.uk/

Other Chapter Books in the Series:

Debbie Duncan, *God Cares When I Am Anxious: Moses and Other Stories*
Debbie Duncan, *God Cares When I Feel Down: Jonah and Other Stories*
Debbie Duncan, *God Cares When Life is Unfair: Joseph and Other Stories*

9 781 78128 376 9

9 781 78128 377 6

9 781 78128 401 8